Partnering with the Holy Spirit

Actively listening to the Holy Spirit and taking action according to what you are hearing

Robert E. Logan

Charles R. Ridley

David J. DeVries

Developed in Partnership

Published by Missional Challenge

Missional Challenge is committed to advancing disciplemaking movements globally.

Visit us at **www.missionalchallenge.com**

ISBN: 978-1-939921-31-4

Acknowledgement

Tara Miller's exceptional writing skills bring our thoughts and ideas to life. Above all others, she makes this book possible. Over many years, her creative collaboration makes it possible to give written resources to the Church so that people can discover and live out their God-given purpose.

CONTENTS

Introduction

God has called—and continues to call—us to a biblical model of discipleship. Discipleship is absolutely foundational to the Vineyard movement. It means following Jesus with all of who we are.

The progression of becoming increasingly more like Jesus—living, loving, serving, helping others become followers of Jesus—is our responsibility as well as our identity as a people.

We live out our discipleship in our words, in our actions, in the presence of community, both those who believe and those who don't.

As disciples on the road to becoming more like Jesus, we yearn for the coming of the Kingdom in all its fullness, the rule and reign of God. We live in the already and the not yet. In community, in scripture, in spiritual formation, in the dynamic work of God among us, we can catch glimpses and tastes of the Kingdom that is yet to come.

As such, we embrace the ongoing process of becoming disciples who make disciples who make disciples. As the yeast mixes through the whole batch of dough, the gospel reproduces itself across the face of the earth. The result is disciples making more disciples making more disciples, then gathering into Kingdom communities called churches.

Discipleship is not something we ever finish in this lifetime. We continue to grow in knowing, being and doing. We progress from an experience of the Holy Spirit, to faith in Jesus, to reconciliation with the Father. We are baptized, we become fishers of men, we obey and teach to obey. We are transformed and transforming. We move toward whole-hearted commitment to God and his Kingdom. The process of discipleship is life-on-life, face-to-face, and hand-in-hand. Together with others, we are invited to join Jesus in the ongoing journey of faith.

Growing in Partnering with the Holy Spirit

Partnering with the Holy Spirit is one of eight discipleship guides for the Vineyard Dimensions of Discipleship series. It doesn't matter which guide you start with—start wherever you'd like and move on to wherever God is leading you next. When we live in the dynamic rhythm and flow of a missional life, we need to take our cues from the Holy Spirit.

These eight guides are organized according to the tree diagram above; examine it to see how all of the pieces fit together. Partnering with the Holy Spirit means actively listening to the Holy Spirit and taking action according to what we are hearing. It connects our experience of God to actions that demonstrate that experience.

Partnering with the Holy Spirit describes how we choose to respond to the work of God in our lives. It involves actively listening and then taking action according to what we are hearing. God is present and at work in the world, drawing us closer to him. How we decide to respond is up to us. Scripture advises us on this count:

"Since we are living by the Spirit, let us follow the Spirit's leading in every part of our lives." Galatians 5:25

"Trust in the Lord with all your heart; do not depend on your own understanding. Seek his will in all you do, and he will show you which path to take." Proverbs 3:5-6

"Do not merely listen to the word, and so deceive yourselves. Do what it says." James 1:22 (NIV)

As God draws near to us through his scriptures, through other people, through the Holy Spirit, what will we do? Will we run and hide, as Adam and Eve did in the garden? Will we step forward in faith even when we don't know what's next, as Abraham did? How will we open ourselves to hearing God's voice and discerning what he is calling us to do? The partnering with the Holy Spirit guide is designed to help us engage questions like these. The following five-part journey covers these five essential expressions of partnering with the Holy Spirit:

- o Increasing ability to hear and discern God's voice

- o Discerning where God is working and actively participating with him o   Checking what you're hearing with scripture and your faith community

o   Risking action in steps of faith and service

o   Discovering your giftedness and calling

> "Being a Christian is less about cautiously avoiding sin than about courageously and actively doing God's will."
> —Dietrich Bonhoeffer

Meet together in a group of three or four to talk through each of these expressions. Ask each other these questions. Wait for and listen to responses from the heart. Encourage, challenge, and affirm one another. Go at your own pace: you can do one a week or one a month, whatever pace works best for you. Be sure to allow enough time to live into these behaviors.

Part 1:

Increasing ability to hear and discern God's voice

Key question: How are you opening yourself up to hearing and discerning God's voice?

We cannot live as we are called to live on our own. We are simply not capable of it. We need the power of the Holy Spirit. Only the Holy Spirit guiding us and speaking to us and empowering us will allow us to respond to what God is calling us to do. We are in a position of need.

How then can we open ourselves to the Holy Spirit? How can we listen for his voice? How can we receive his power? We need to come to God in prayer with a spirit of humility and supplication, recognizing that without the power of the Spirit, we cannot live out what God has called us toward. That power is how the early church was built and how the church continues to be built—through our receiving guidance and empowerment from the Spirit.

When we hear the Spirit calling us to do something, we need to step forward in faith and do it, relying on God to see it through. We can do all things through Christ, who strengths us (Philippians 4:13).

"If God can work through me, he can work through anyone."
—Saint Francis of Assisi

Prayer

Ask God to fill you with his power and his Spirit. Ask him to guide you toward what he wants you to do. Ask him to give you a listening ear for his voice and a willing heart to obey it. Then wait in a posture of attentiveness.

This week read and reflect daily on the scripture below. Open a natural flow of conversational prayer with the Holy Spirit as you meditate on the scriptures, inviting him to reveal himself to you. Then gather with those who journey alongside you and interact over the discipleship questions.

Luke 24:49

[49] "And now I will send the Holy Spirit, just as my Father promised. But stay here in the city until the Holy Spirit comes and fills you with power from heaven."

Acts 2:1-21

On the day of Pentecost all the believers were meeting together in one place. [2] Suddenly, there was a sound from heaven like the roaring of a mighty windstorm, and it filled the house where they were sitting. [3] Then, what looked like flames or tongues of fire appeared and settled on each of them. [4] And everyone present was filled with the Holy Spirit and began speaking in other languages, as the Holy Spirit gave them this ability.

[5] At that time there were devout Jews from every nation living in Jerusalem. [6] When they heard the loud noise, everyone came running, and they were bewildered to hear their own languages being spoken by the believers.

[7] They were completely amazed. "How can this be?" they exclaimed. "These people are all from Galilee, [8] and yet we hear them speaking in our own native languages! [9] Here we are—Parthians, Medes, Elamites, people from Mesopotamia, Judea,

Cappadocia, Pontus, the province of Asia, ¹⁰ Phrygia, Pamphylia, Egypt, and the areas of Libya around Cyrene, visitors from Rome ¹¹ (both Jews and converts to Judaism), Cretans, and Arabs. And we all hear these people speaking in our own languages about the wonderful things God has done!" ¹² They stood there amazed and perplexed. "What can this mean?" they asked each other.

¹³ But others in the crowd ridiculed them, saying, "They're just drunk, that's all!"

¹⁴ Then Peter stepped forward with the eleven other apostles and shouted to the crowd, "Listen carefully, all of you, fellow Jews and residents of Jerusalem! Make no mistake about this. ¹⁵ These people are not drunk, as some of you are assuming. Nine o'clock in the morning is much too early for that. ¹⁶ No, what you see was predicted long ago by the prophet Joel:

¹⁷ 'In the last days,' God says,
   'I will pour out my Spirit upon all people.
Your sons and daughters will prophesy.
   Your young men will see visions,
   and your old men will dream dreams.
¹⁸ In those days I will pour out my Spirit
   even on my servants—men and women alike—
   and they will prophesy.
¹⁹ And I will cause wonders in the heavens above
   and signs on the earth below—
   blood and fire and clouds of smoke.
²⁰ The sun will become dark,
   and the moon will turn blood red
   before that great and glorious day of the LORD arrives.
²¹ But everyone who calls on the name of the LORD
   will be saved.'

———————————

Discipleship questions:

o   When have you been most aware of hearing God's voice?

o   How are you relying on the Holy Spirit?

o   How are you waiting for him?

o   What are you hearing from the Holy Spirit? How are you listening?

o   What do you really want God to empower you to do?

- How can you pray for one another as you wait to receive guidance and empowerment from the Spirit?

Action steps:

- In light of this, what is God asking you to do?

- How will you do this?

- When will you do this?

- Who will help you?

Part 2:

Discerning where God is working and actively participating with him

Key question: *Where—and in whom—do you see God working? How can you join him in what he is doing?*

One of the most powerful recognitions we can have as we respond to the leading of God is that he has already gone before us. We are not alone; he already sent his Holy Spirit to prepare the way. He calls us to be faithful, to do what we can with what we have, but the results of our faithfulness do not lie with us. God is already at work in others long before we come on the scene. He chooses to use us and work through us. Part of our faithfulness is simply paying attention to what God is already doing and following his lead.

> "Stop asking God to bless what you're doing. Find out what God's doing. It's already blessed." —Bono

God is at work everywhere—all around us. Look around you. Where can you see him at work? What evidence has he left behind? Where do you sense openness to his Spirit? What questions are people asking?

This week read and reflect daily on the scripture below. Open a natural flow of conversational prayer with the Holy Spirit as you meditate on the scriptures, inviting him to reveal himself to you. Then gather with those who journey alongside you and interact over the discipleship questions.

John 5:16-23

16 So the Jewish leaders began harassing Jesus for breaking the Sabbath rules. 17 But Jesus replied, "My Father is always working, and so am I." 18 So the Jewish leaders tried all the harder to find a way to kill him. For he not only broke the Sabbath, he called God his Father, thereby making himself equal with God.

19 So Jesus explained, "I tell you the truth, the Son can do nothing by himself. He does only what he sees the Father doing. Whatever the Father does, the Son also does. 20 For the Father loves the Son and shows him everything he is doing. In fact, the Father will show him how to do even greater works than healing this man. Then you will truly be astonished. 21 For just as the Father gives life to those he raises from the dead, so the Son gives life to anyone he wants. 22 In addition, the Father judges no one. Instead, he has given the Son absolute authority to judge, 23 so that everyone will honor the Son, just as they honor the Father. Anyone who does not honor the Son is certainly not honoring the Father who sent him.

Luke 19:1-7

Jesus entered Jericho and made his way through the town. 2 There was a man there named Zacchaeus. He was the chief tax collector in the region, and he had become very rich. 3 He tried to get a look at Jesus, but he was too short to see over the crowd. 4 So he ran ahead and climbed a sycamore-fig tree beside the road, for Jesus was going to pass that way.

5 When Jesus came by, he looked up at Zacchaeus and called him by name. "Zacchaeus!" he said. "Quick, come down! I must be a guest in your home today."

6 Zacchaeus quickly climbed down and took Jesus to his house in great excitement and joy. 7 But the people were displeased. "He has gone to be the guest of a notorious sinner," they grumbled.

Discipleship questions:

- ○ God is at work everywhere—but where are you currently most sensing his presence and work?

- ○ What are some of the different ways God communicates that he's at work somewhere?

- ○ What are some of the signs of openness we can see in people?

- ○ What are some of the ways we can engage with those who are searching for God?

- ○ Where do you sense God working right now?

Expression through art

Create a painting or drawing that represents to you how you see God at work in the world.

Action steps:

- In light of this, what is God asking you to do?

- How will you do this?

- When will you do this?

- Who will help you?

Part 3:

Checking what you're hearing with scripture and your faith community

Key question: What do you need to check with scripture and your community?

It's possible we might think we hear God telling us to jump off a bridge. That's why we need to check what we're hearing with scripture and also with our faith community. We don't always hear accurately. If we think we are hearing something that doesn't align with scripture, it's not from God. Don't forget to check what you are hearing against the Word of God, where we know God is speaking.

One thing we also forget on a regular basis is that we need other people. We might remember at breakfast, then forget again by 9:00am. We keep thinking we should be able to do everything on our own, and this stubborn belief certainly extends to what we are hearing from God. When we believe we are hearing something from God, after checking scripture, then the next step is to see if other people are hearing the same thing. Does it line up with what others are hearing? Do others have a perspective on what we're hearing that could be helpful to us? When God is truly at work, he most often orchestrates things so we are not alone in responding to him. We need other people.

> "Anyone who doesn't take truth seriously in small matters cannot be trusted in large ones either." —Albert Einstein

This week read and reflect daily on the scripture below. Open a natural flow of conversational prayer with the Holy Spirit as you meditate on the scriptures, inviting him to reveal himself to you. Then gather with those who journey alongside you and interact over the discipleship questions.

Acts 17:10-12

[10] As soon as it was night, the believers sent Paul and Silas away to Berea. On arriving there, they went to the Jewish synagogue. [11] Now the Berean Jews were of more noble character than those in Thessalonica, for they received the message with great eagerness and examined the Scriptures every day to see if what Paul said was true. [12] Many of them believed, as did also a number of prominent Greek women and many Greek men. (NIV)

Acts 6:1-7

But as the believers rapidly multiplied, there were rumblings of discontent. The Greek-speaking believers complained about the Hebrew-speaking believers, saying that their widows were being discriminated against in the daily distribution of food.

[2] So the Twelve called a meeting of all the believers. They said, "We apostles should spend our time teaching the word of God, not running a food program. [3] And so, brothers, select seven men who are well respected and are full of the Spirit and wisdom. We will give them this responsibility. [4] Then we apostles can spend our time in prayer and teaching the word."

[5] Everyone liked this idea, and they chose the following: Stephen (a man full of faith and the Holy Spirit), Philip, Procorus, Nicanor, Timon, Parmenas, and Nicolas of Antioch (an earlier convert to the Jewish faith). [6] These seven were presented to the apostles, who prayed for them as they laid their hands on them.

[7] So God's message continued to spread. The number of believers greatly increased in Jerusalem, and many of the Jewish priests were converted, too.

Discipleship questions:

- How do you know when you are hearing from God?

- What kinds of "checks" do you perform to see if you are hearing correctly?

- Who do you regularly talk with about what you're hearing from God?

- How do you use scripture to help you make decisions?

○ Tell about a time when what you heard from God did not seem to have the backing of your community. How did you navigate that?

Ask three

Ask three people you trust to give you honest, open feedback about what you are hearing from God. Try not to become defensive: just listen. Ask follow up questions as necessary.

Action steps:

○ In light of this, what is God asking you to do?

○ How will you do this?

o   When will you do this?

o   Who will help you?

Part 4:

Risking action in steps of faith and service

Key question: How are you stepping forward in faith?

The true test of faith is action. Hearing from God matters not at all if we are unwilling to take steps based on what we are hearing. Just as knowledge without putting it to use is void, so is hearing from God and ignoring what he is telling us.

"God doesn't require us to succeed; he only requires that you try." —Mother Teresa

Admittedly, this is easier said than done. There is almost always some element of risk in our obedience, and that risk can range all to the way from martyrdom to looking like a fool. The question is this: What is more important to us… obeying what we are hearing from God or our own self-interests? Our answer to this question is not theoretical; it is borne out in our actions.

This week read and reflect daily on the scripture below. Open a natural flow of conversational prayer with the Holy Spirit as you meditate on the scriptures, inviting him to reveal himself to you. Then gather with those who journey alongside you and interact over the discipleship questions.

Matthew 9:35-38

[35] Jesus traveled through all the towns and villages of that area, teaching in the synagogues and announcing the Good News about the Kingdom. And he healed every kind of disease and illness. [36] When he saw the crowds, he had compassion on

them because they were confused and helpless, like sheep without a shepherd. **37** He said to his disciples, "The harvest is great, but the workers are few. **38** So pray to the Lord who is in charge of the harvest; ask him to send more workers into his fields...."

Matthew 10:5-8

5 Jesus sent out the twelve apostles with these instructions: "Don't go to the Gentiles or the Samaritans, **6** but only to the people of Israel—God's lost sheep. **7** Go and announce to them that the Kingdom of Heaven is near. **8** Heal the sick, raise the dead, cure those with leprosy, and cast out demons. Give as freely as you have received!

Hebrews 11

Faith is the confidence that what we hope for will actually happen; it gives us assurance about things we cannot see. **2** Through their faith, the people in days of old earned a good reputation.

3 By faith we understand that the entire universe was formed at God's command, that what we now see did not come from anything that can be seen. **4** It was by faith that Abel brought a more acceptable offering to God than Cain did. Abel's offering gave evidence that he was a righteous man, and God showed his approval of his gifts. Although Abel is long dead, he still speaks to us by his example of faith.

5 It was by faith that Enoch was taken up to heaven without dying—"he disappeared, because God took him." For before he was taken up, he was known as a person who pleased God. **6** And it is impossible to please God without faith. Anyone who wants to come to him must believe that God exists and that he rewards those who sincerely seek him.

7 It was by faith that Noah built a large boat to save his family from the flood. He obeyed God, who warned him about things that had never happened before. By his faith Noah condemned the rest of the world, and he received the righteousness that comes by faith.

[8] It was by faith that Abraham obeyed when God called him to leave home and go to another land that God would give him as his inheritance. He went without knowing where he was going. [9] And even when he reached the land God promised him, he lived there by faith—for he was like a foreigner, living in tents. And so did Isaac and Jacob, who inherited the same promise. [10] Abraham was confidently looking forward to a city with eternal foundations, a city designed and built by God.

[11] It was by faith that even Sarah was able to have a child, though she was barren and was too old. She believed that God would keep his promise. [12] And so a whole nation came from this one man who was as good as dead—a nation with so many people that, like the stars in the sky and the sand on the seashore, there is no way to count them.

[13] All these people died still believing what God had promised them. They did not receive what was promised, but they saw it all from a distance and welcomed it. They agreed that they were foreigners and nomads here on earth. [14] Obviously people who say such things are looking forward to a country they can call their own. [15] If they had longed for the country they came from, they could have gone back. [16] But they were looking for a better place, a heavenly homeland. That is why God is not ashamed to be called their God, for he has prepared a city for them.

[17] It was by faith that Abraham offered Isaac as a sacrifice when God was testing him. Abraham, who had received God's promises, was ready to sacrifice his only son, Isaac, [18] even though God had told him, "Isaac is the son through whom your descendants will be counted." [19] Abraham reasoned that if Isaac died, God was able to bring him back to life again. And in a sense, Abraham did receive his son back from the dead.

[20] It was by faith that Isaac promised blessings for the future to

his sons, Jacob and Esau.

21 It was by faith that Jacob, when he was old and dying, blessed each of Joseph's sons and bowed in worship as he leaned on his staff.

22 It was by faith that Joseph, when he was about to die, said confidently that the people of Israel would leave Egypt. He even commanded them to take his bones with them when they left.

23 It was by faith that Moses' parents hid him for three months when he was born. They saw that God had given them an unusual child, and they were not afraid to disobey the king's command.

24 It was by faith that Moses, when he grew up, refused to be called the son of Pharaoh's daughter. 25 He chose to share the oppression of God's people instead of enjoying the fleeting pleasures of sin. 26 He thought it was better to suffer for the sake of Christ than to own the treasures of Egypt, for he was looking ahead to his great reward. 27 It was by faith that Moses left the land of Egypt, not fearing the king's anger. He kept right on going because he kept his eyes on the one who is invisible. 28 It was by faith that Moses commanded the people of Israel to keep the Passover and to sprinkle blood on the doorposts so that the angel of death would not kill their firstborn sons.

29 It was by faith that the people of Israel went right through the Red Sea as though they were on dry ground. But when the Egyptians tried to follow, they were all drowned.

30 It was by faith that the people of Israel marched around Jericho for seven days, and the walls came crashing down.

31 It was by faith that Rahab the prostitute was not destroyed with the people in her city who refused to obey God. For she had given a friendly welcome to the spies.

32 How much more do I need to say? It would take too long to recount the stories of the faith of Gideon, Barak, Samson,

Jephthah, David, Samuel, and all the prophets. [33] By faith these people overthrew kingdoms, ruled with justice, and received what God had promised them. They shut the mouths of lions, [34] quenched the flames of fire, and escaped death by the edge of the sword. Their weakness was turned to strength. They became strong in battle and put whole armies to flight. [35] Women received their loved ones back again from death.

But others were tortured, refusing to turn from God in order to be set free. They placed their hope in a better life after the resurrection. [36] Some were jeered at, and their backs were cut open with whips. Others were chained in prisons. [37] Some died by stoning, some were sawed in half, and others were killed with the sword. Some went about wearing skins of sheep and goats, destitute and oppressed and mistreated. [38] They were too good for this world, wandering over deserts and mountains, hiding in caves and holes in the ground.

[39] All these people earned a good reputation because of their faith, yet none of them received all that God had promised. [40] For God had something better in mind for us, so that they would not reach perfection without us.

Discipleship questions:

- Tell about a time when you felt God was asking you to do something that made you afraid. What happened?

o How do you imagine the disciples felt when Jesus sent them out?

o How did they then go on to proclaim and demonstrate the reality of the Kingdom?

o What are some steps of faith that you have seen God call you or others to take?

o When is obedience hardest for you? When is obedience easiest?

o What actions do you feel God might be calling you toward? How do you feel about that?

Action steps:

- ○ In light of this, what is God asking you to do?

- ○ How will you do this?

- ○ When will you do this?

- ○ Who will help you?

Part 5:

Discovering your giftedness and calling

Key question: *How are you discovering your giftedness and calling?*

One of the beauties of the Vineyard movement was summed up by John Wimber: "Everybody gets to play." Ministry is not limited to the few: it's for all of us. God wants all of us to discovery our giftedness and calling and to use those for the benefit of others.

The term "calling" has been interpreted many different ways. Many believers have spent years disengaged from ministry while waiting for a supernatural communication from God. Sometimes God gives those types of miraculous signs: the apostle Paul was practically struck by lightning and told what to do with the rest of his life. However, that's not the case for most of us. Yet that doesn't mean we don't have a calling; it just means we have a different way of finding that calling.

God has something for every believer to do in this life. We all have spiritual gifts that God expects us to exercise. We all have a contribution to make toward the coming of his Kingdom. Our task is to listen to God's voice, to live in obedience to the commands God has given all people, and to discern as we go what else God would have us do. We are to use the gifts we have and trust that God will continue to lead us. Even if we don't have a clear direction, we are still to be in motion. The basic principles of motion are that an object in motion tends to stay in motion, and an object at rest tends to stay at rest.

> An object in motion tends to remain in motion, and an object at rest tends to remain at rest. — Isaac Newton, first law of motion

As we move forward in obedience to what we already know to do, more direction will be given to us by the Holy Spirit.

This week read and reflect daily on the scripture below. Open a natural flow of conversational prayer with the Holy Spirit as you meditate on the scriptures, inviting him to reveal himself to you. Then gather with those who journey alongside you and interact over the discipleship questions.

Matthew 4:18-20

[18] One day as Jesus was walking along the shore of the Sea of Galilee, he saw two brothers—Simon, also called Peter, and Andrew—throwing a net into the water, for they fished for a living. [19] Jesus called out to them, "Come, follow me, and I will show you how to fish for people!" [20] And they left their nets at once and followed him.

Mark 5:18-20

[18] As Jesus was getting into the boat, the man who had been demon possessed begged to go with him. [19] But Jesus said, "No, go home to your family, and tell them everything the Lord has done for you and how merciful he has been." [20] So the man started off to visit the Ten Towns of that region and began to proclaim the great things Jesus had done for him; and everyone was amazed at what he told them.

Ephesians 4:1-6

Therefore I, a prisoner for serving the Lord, beg you to lead a life worthy of your calling, for you have been called by God. [2] Always be humble and gentle. Be patient with each other, making allowance for each other's faults because of your love.

[3] Make every effort to keep yourselves united in the Spirit, binding yourselves together with peace. [4] For there is one body and one Spirit, just as you have been called to one glorious hope for the future. [5] There is one Lord, one faith, one baptism, [6] and one God and Father, who is over all and in all and living through all.

Philippians 3:12-14

[12] I don't mean to say that I have already achieved these things or that I have already reached perfection. But I press on to possess that perfection for which Christ Jesus first possessed me. [13] No, dear brothers and sisters, I have not achieved it, but I focus on this one thing: Forgetting the past and looking forward to what lies ahead, [14] I press on to reach the end of the race and receive the heavenly prize for which God, through Christ Jesus, is calling us.

1 Timothy 6:12

[12] Fight the good fight for the true faith. Hold tightly to the eternal life to which God has called you, which you have confessed so well before many witnesses.

"A dead thing goes with the stream, but only a living thing can go against it." —G.K. Chesterton, *The Everlasting Man*

Discipleship questions:

○ What spiritual gifts has God given you? How are you exercising those?

o   How do you understand God's call for your life?

o   What are some of the things he calls all believers to?

o   How will you discern those things he is calling you specifically to?

o   What practices can help you seek out God's calling in your life?

o   How do God's calling and your desires fit together?

Exercise: What do you already know God wants you to do? Search the scriptures for commands. Write down as many as you can.

Action steps:

○   In light of this, what is God asking you to do?

○   How will you do this?

○   When will you do this?

○   Who will help you?

What's next?

So you've completed this guide. What now? Is there another dimension of discipleship you need to zoom in on? If so, which one?

Because the Vineyard Dimensions of Discipleship guides aren't meant to be used in any particular order, it's up to you to do some listening to the Holy Spirit. Take a look at the big picture and decide where God is leading you next. With a holistic system, it's always a surprise. No matter which guide you choose next, you're engaged in an ongoing action-reflection process as you continue living incarnationally and missionally. All of the Vineyard Dimensions of Discipleship guides are listed below:

- *Experiencing and Worshipping God:* Intentionally and consistently engaging with God in such a way that you open yourself to a deeper relationship with him and his Kingdom

- *Partnering with the Holy Spirit:* Actively listening to the Holy Spirit and taking action according to what you are hearing

- *Sacrificial Service:* Doing good works out of the overflow of God's love and work in our lives

- *Generous Living:* Faithfully stewarding and investing what God has given you so you can contribute toward the advancement of the Kingdom

- *Disciplemaking:* Living in obedience to the great commission given by Jesus, which entails making more and better followers of Christ

- *Personal Transformation:* Experiencing change in your attitudes and behaviors as a result of your relationship with God and others

- *Authentic Relationships:* Engaging with other people in ways that reflect the heart of God toward them

- *Community Transformation:* Personal involvement with others to facilitate positive change where you live and beyond

Maybe what's next isn't another Vineyard Dimensions of Discipleship guide. Here are a few other options:

- If you have a friend or mentor you've been going through these guides with—or if you'd like to begin

- o discipling someone, you can greatly increase the fruitfulness of your coaching relationship using www.disciple.mycoachlog.com—a tool to help you stay on track, reflect on what God is doing, and celebrate progress.

- o You may be ready to take coaching to the next level by getting a coach, being trained as a coach, or having coach training facilitated for your church. Check out www.missionaltoolkit.com/coaching for more information about these opportunities.

- o You can move on to a similar series: The Journey Together Now guides. You can find out more about these downloadable guides at www.journeytogethernow.com.

No matter what's next for you, continue to grow in the ways you follow Jesus into your continuing journey of discipleship.

VINEYARD
DISCIPLE
ASSESSMENT

Advancing your spiritual development

vineyard.discipleassessment.com

Your church will only grow as well as the disciples that you develop.

Finally - a way to measure progress in discipleship reliably:
for individuals, small groups, churches, and missional communities.

The portrait of Jesus in the four gospels serves as our guide.
Disciples seek to live and love like Jesus.

The **Vineyard Disciple Assessment** provides a snapshot of where
you are in 8 dimensions of following Jesus.

Benefits to your Ministry:

- Every believer discovers growth areas

- Intentional, reproducible discipleship process

- Encourages everyone to live and love like Jesus

- Relational, Spirit-led context for moving forward

- Development of more and better disciples

This **360° assessment** provides feedback that can help you see your own path of discipleship more accurately and more holistically, as well as provide direction for future growth. Your view along with the perspective of friends, family, spiritual leaders, and those you are influencing to follow Jesus will give you **comprehensive feedback on your progress as a disciple.**

Dimensions of Discipleship

*After taking the Vineyard Disciple Assessment—
discover ways to grow deeper through the
Vineyard Dimensions of Discipleship Guides
and e-courses.*

Go to vineyard.discipleassessment.com/resources today.

Made in the USA
San Bernardino, CA
22 May 2015